Enrichment

READING

Peggy Kaye

IV

III

CL

Dear Student,

   Here is your very own *Enrichment Reading* book. The book is filled with exciting reading things to do at home. In it you will find games, contests, puzzles, riddles, information, stories, and all sorts of surprises. Best of all, you may ask your family or friends to work on the activities with you.

   While you are having fun, you will be doing a lot of reading. You will also be learning how exciting reading can be.

   Your friends at *Enrichment Reading* hope this book will be one of your favorite things to do. Good luck and happy reading!

I

II

VI

Contents

1 Word Detective

List eight objects you find in your classroom or your home.
Next to each object, write the first describing word you think
of when you look at the object.
Then write a word that means the same or almost the same
as the describing word.
Finally, write a word that means the opposite of the
describing word.

Object	Describing Word	Same	Opposite
table	hard	solid	soft
1.			
2.			
3.			
4.			
5.			
6.			
7.			
8.			

Wonder Wheel

Here is a game to play with an adult.
Make ten word cards like these.
Put the cards in a pile and turn the pile face down.
Take the top card and read the word.
Then toss a penny onto the Wonder Wheel.
If it lands on **S**, say a word that means the same as the word on the card.
If it lands on **O**, say a word that means the opposite of the word on the card.
If both players agree a word is right, score 5 points.
Then return the card to the bottom of the pile.
Take turns and keep score on a piece of paper.
Play until one player scores 30 points.

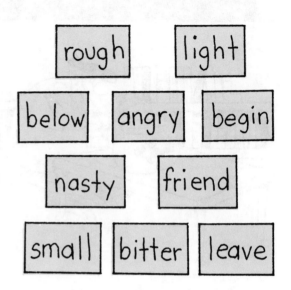

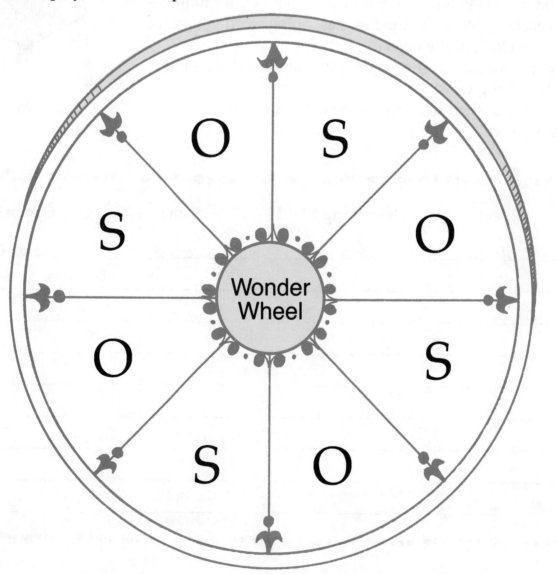

2 Jungle Maze

Help the explorer find her way through the jungle.
Use a pencil to follow the path of words with prefixes.
Be careful, or the explorer will be lost forever.

triangle

thunderstorm

redo

mammal

invisible

return

discover

hunter

export

offshore

subway

native

bicycle

recall

bypass

unable

message

animal

unlock

pathway

original

tiger

sunrise

tricornered

bilevel

infield

hungry

discontinue

uncertain

misdirect

territory

project

prepay

dislike

recount

marsh

uncover

kidnap

reappear

precooked

Prefix Puzzle

Ask someone to play this game with you.
Toss a penny or paper clip onto the puzzle.
Read the word on which it lands.
If the word has one prefix, score 5 points.
If the word has two prefixes, score 10 points.
If the word has no prefixes, your score is 0.
Take turns and play six rounds. Keep score below.
The player with the higher score wins.

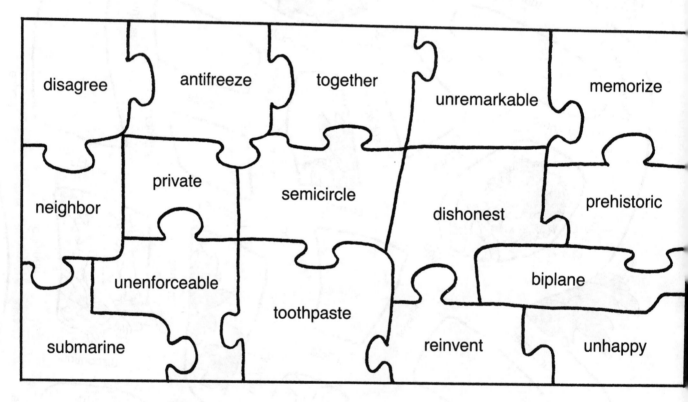

Score Sheet	
Player 1	**Player 2**
Round 1	Round 1
Round 2	Round 2
Round 3	Round 3
Round 4	Round 4
Round 5	Round 5
Round 6	Round 6
TOTAL	TOTAL

3 ▷ Message Wall

The bricklayer needs help completing the message on the wall.
Each brick on the ground contains a different suffix.
Write the correct suffix in each empty space.
Cross out the suffix after you use it.

To	beauti		your	block	you	do	not
need	a	paint		or	magic		Just
work	out	a	reason		plan	that	will
keep	your	neighbor		clean,	not	mess	

| able | fy | er | y | hood | ian |

What does the message say?
List three things for a plan to keep your neighborhood clean.

_____

_____

_____

Did You Know?

Play this game with a friend or an adult.
Make eight suffix cards like these.

| est | ance | ly | ing | ment | y | less | ed |

Turn the cards face down.
Choose a card.
If the suffix on the card completes the unfinished word in
one of your sentences, write the suffix on the blank and keep
the card.
If you cannot use the suffix, turn the card back over.
Take turns.
The first player to complete all four sentences is the winner.

Player 1 _____

The discover_____ of dinosaur
bones in England in 1822 was a great
surprise.

The fear_____ Tyrannosaurs were
savage meat eaters.

Scientists general_____ agree that
dinosaurs are more closely related to
birds than to reptiles.

The disappear_____ of dinosaurs
may have been caused by a change in
the earth's climate.

Player 2 _____

There is disagree_____ on
whether dinosaurs were cold-blooded,
like reptiles, or warm-blooded, like
birds.

The long_____ known dinosaur
to ever live was 90 feet long.

Scientists learn about dinosaurs by
study_____ the preserved bones,
teeth, eggs, and tracks of dinosaurs.

Some museums have create_____
realistic models of dinosaurs out of
metal, wire, and screen.

Name _____

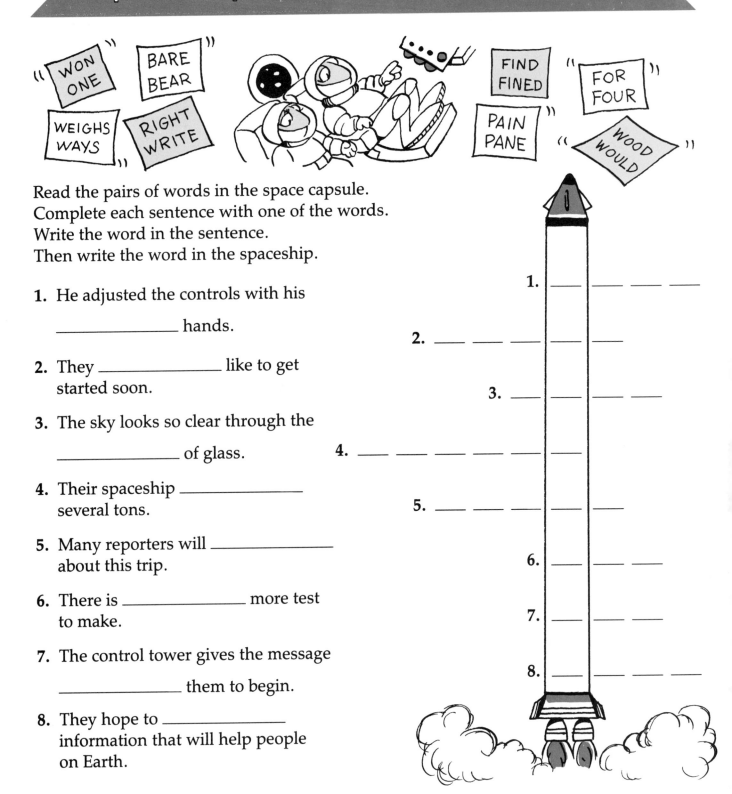

Read the pairs of words in the space capsule.
Complete each sentence with one of the words.
Write the word in the sentence.
Then write the word in the spaceship.

1. He adjusted the controls with his

   _____ hands.

2. They _____ like to get
   started soon.

3. The sky looks so clear through the

   _____ of glass.

4. Their spaceship _____
   several tons.

5. Many reporters will _____
   about this trip.

6. There is _____ more test
   to make.

7. The control tower gives the message

   _____ them to begin.

8. They hope to _____
   information that will help people
   on Earth.

1. ___ ___ ___ ___
2. ___ ___ ___ ___
3. ___ ___ ___
4. ___ ___ ___ ___ ___
5. ___ ___ ___ ___
6. ___ ___ ___
7. ___ ___ ___
8. ___ ___ ___ ___ ___

Read down on the spaceship.
What are the astronauts going to do now? _____

Ask and Answer

This is a game to play with a friend.
Use small pieces of paper to make six sets of word cards like these.

| rain | reign |

| brakes | breaks | | cent | scent | | main | mane | | pail | pale |

| steal | steel |

Each player gets one card from each set.
Take turns.
Close your eyes and put a finger on the game board.
Read the question you are pointing to.
If you have the right word to answer the question, tape the word card over the question on the board.
If you point to a question that is already answered, take another turn.
Keep playing until all the questions are answered.

How might a frightened person look?	What do you use to stop a car?	What is another name for a penny?
What is the period during which a queen or king rules?	What does a thief do?	What is the largest or most important street in a town?
What do we call the smell of a flower?	What is a round container for carrying water?	What happens to a glass that falls to the floor?
What is the long hair on the back of a lion called?	What falls from the clouds during a storm?	What material is used to build the frame of a tall building?

Name _____

 Riddles

A riddle is a question with a tricky answer.
Read each riddle below.
Choose one of the words under the blank to complete the answer.
Write the word you choose on the blank.
Compare your completed riddles with your classmates.
Discuss how each answer is tricky.

1. If you put several ducks in a box, what do you have?

   A box of _____.
   crackers   quackers

2. How did the rocket lose its job?

   It was _____.
   fired   tired

3. What is a good way to keep a dog off the street?

   Put it in a _____ lot.
   parking   barking

4. Why can't I make a phone call to the zoo?

   The _____ are busy.
   lines   lions

5. Would you like some more alphabet soup?

   No, I can't eat another _____.
   syllable   spoonful

6. What is a mosquito's favorite sport?

   Skin _____.
   diving   driving

7. Why is tennis such a noisy game?

   Each player raises a _____.
   rattle   racket

8. What animals need to be oiled?

   Mice, because they _____.
   squeak   speak

9. What is an astronaut sandwich made of?

   _____ meat.
   Lunch   Launch

What Does It Mean?

Do this activity with an adult.
Read what the scientists are saying in each cartoon picture.
Work together.
Decide what you think the word in dark print means.
Write the meaning of the word below the picture.

Name _____

6 Color Your Sentences

A colorful description compares two things in an unusual way.
For each box, read the sentence beginnings on the left.
Then read the sentence endings on the right.
Draw a line from the beginning of each sentence to the
ending that makes the best colorful description.

Her eyes were	as heavy as rocks.
The kangaroo jumped	as big as pizzas.
The boxes were	as high as the stars.

The thirsty boy	looks like diamonds.
The motor	sounds like a hive of bees.
The light on the water	drank like a fish.

The ticking clock is	a time bomb.
The little puppy is	an oven.
This room is	a real clown.

Look around your classroom or your home.

Find something that is *as red as a beet.* _____

Think of something that is *a walking encyclopedia.* _____

Look for something that *walks like an elephant.* _____

Now use your imagination to complete these sentences.

_____ as loud as thunder.

_____ is a grumpy old bear.

_____ like a shooting star.

Completing similes and metaphors **13**

What's It Like?

This is a game for two players.
Make ten word cards like these.

| spider | earthquake | ice cube | trumpet | microphone |

| moon | dream | marshmallow | rainbow | chimpanzee |

Put the cards face down.
Take turns.
Select one card.
Read the word on the card to yourself.
Then describe the object on the card by answering each
question on the Question Board.
Try to use colorful descriptions.
If the other player guesses what the object is, keep the card.
If the player does not guess the object, return the card face down.
Play until there are no more words left to describe.

Question Board

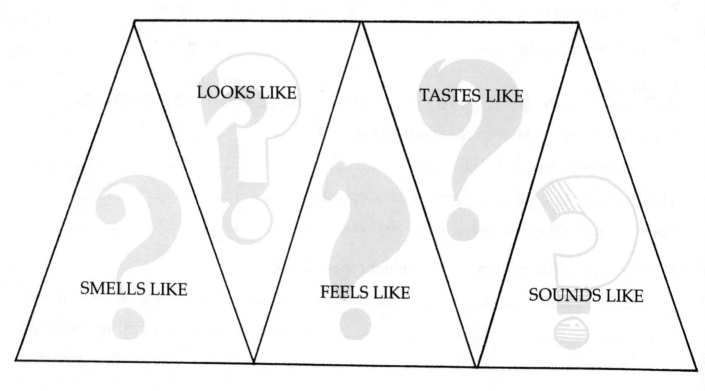

LOOKS LIKE

TASTES LIKE

SMELLS LIKE

FEELS LIKE

SOUNDS LIKE

7 Crosswords

Read each clue.
Decide what word completes the sentence and fits in the crossword puzzle.
Write the answer in the puzzle.

ACROSS

1. *Finger* is to _____ as *toe* is to *foot*.

4. _____ is to *out* as *up* is to *down*.

7. *Shoes* are to *feet* as _____ are to *hands*.

9. *Snow* is to *cold* as _____ is to *hot*.

10. *Minute* is to *hour* as *day* is to _____.

11. *Water* is to _____ as *air* is to *airplane*.

13. *Brother* is to *boy* as _____ is to *girl*.

15. *Easy* is to _____ as *hard* is to *difficult*.

DOWN

2. *Library* is to *books* as *cupboard* is to _____.

3. _____ is to *bed* as *sit* is to *chair*.

5. *Brake* is to *stop* as _____ is to *go*.

6. *Fruit* is to *apple* as *vegetable* is to _____.

8. *Dog* is to _____ as *bird* is to *chirps*.

9. *Broom* is to _____ as *pen* is to *write*.

10. *Penny* is to *dollar* as *foot* is to _____.

12. _____ is to *skate* as *water* is to *swim*.

14. *One* is to _____ as *three* is to *four*.

Ladder Climb

Play this game with an adult.
Use long narrow strips of paper to make twelve word cards
like these.

| breakfast |

| brush | | hear | | clean | | time | | sing |

| write | | country | | insect | | king | | fins |

Turn the cards face down.
Choose a card. Read the word on it.
If the word on the card answers one of the questions on your
ladder, tape the card below the question.
If you cannot use the card, turn it back over.
Take turns.
The first player to complete a ladder wins the game.

| shape |

Player 1

If eyes look, what do ears do?

If a robin is a bird, what is a beetle?

If you read a story, what do you do
with a song?

If you comb your hair, what do you do
to your teeth?

If a princess may become queen,
what might a prince become?

If mud makes you dirty, what does
soap make you?

Player 2

If a dog has paws, what does a fish
have?

If a calendar tells the date, what does
a clock tell?

If you draw with a crayon, what do you
do with a pencil?

If blue is a color, what is a circle?

If you eat dinner in the evening, what
do you eat in the morning?

If Ohio is a state, what is the United
States?

Wagon Wheels

8

Read the group of words on each wheel.
In the center, write a name for the group.

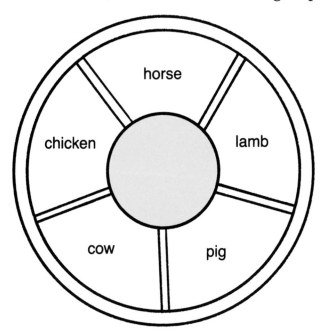

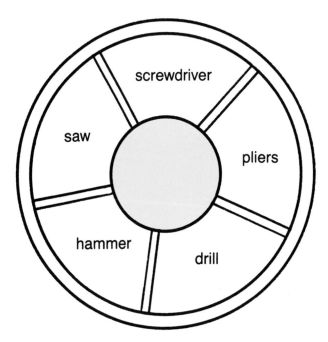

Read the group name in the center of the first wheel.
Complete the wheel with words that belong in the group.
Then do the second wheel.
Fill in the name of a group and five words that belong in it.

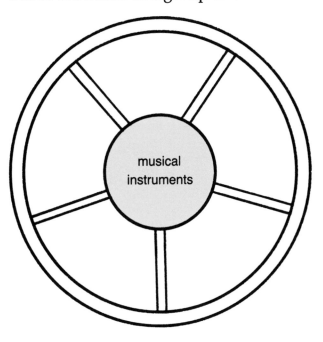

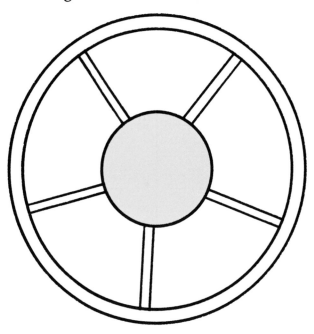

List Five

This is an activity for you to do with a friend or family member.
Work together.
Choose four boxes and write the box numbers on the chart below.
Then complete the chart by listing the things asked for in the boxes.
Try to list the most unusual things you can think of.
Take your chart to school tomorrow and compare your lists
with your classmates' lists.

1 five things in your home that run on electricity	2 five things an elephant might think about	3 five ways a snowball feels	4 five things you can do with your eyes
5 five things a kangaroo could learn in school	6 five ways a rainbow looks	7 five things a robot would like to eat	8 five things you can do with a skateboard

Box _____   Box _____   Box _____   Box _____

1. _____   1. _____   1. _____   1. _____

2. _____   2. _____   2. _____   2. _____

3. _____   3. _____   3. _____   3. _____

4. _____   4. _____   4. _____   4. _____

5. _____   5. _____   5. _____   5. _____

Name _____

Read the word that goes down the side of the page.
What other words does it make you think of?
Write three words on the blanks after each letter.
The words must begin with the letter at the beginning of the row.
When you are finished, you will have a funny word poem.
Practice reading your poem to yourself.
Write a title for your poem on the line above it.
Then read your poem out loud to your friends, classmates,
and family.

_____

M _merry_ _____ _____

O _____ _____ _____

N _____ _____ _____

S _____ _____ _____

T _____ _____ _____

E _____ _____ _____

R _____ _____ _____

Try writing another poem on a separate piece of paper.
Write your name or a favorite word down the side.
Then complete the poem as you did above.

One Word Leads to Another

Do this activity with an adult.
What words does each picture make you think of?
Follow the arrows and take turns adding words.
Continue until all the blanks around each picture are filled.
Then read the words around each picture to a friend or
family member.
See if he or she can guess what the picture is.

start

around →

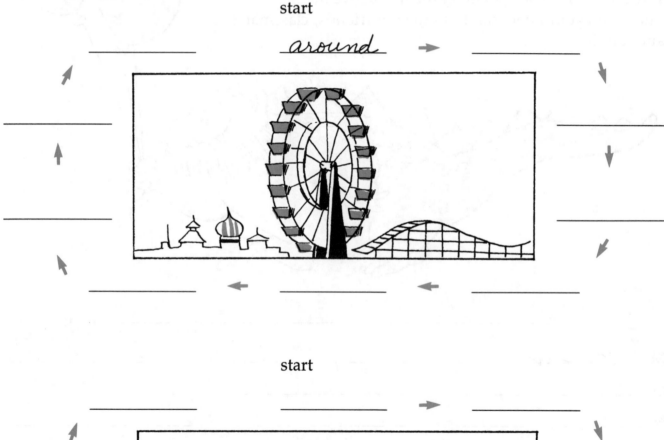

start

Name _____

10 How Many?

Read each word.
Color all one syllable words orange.
Color all two syllable words yellow.
Color all three syllable words green.
Color all four syllable words blue.
Color all five syllable words red.

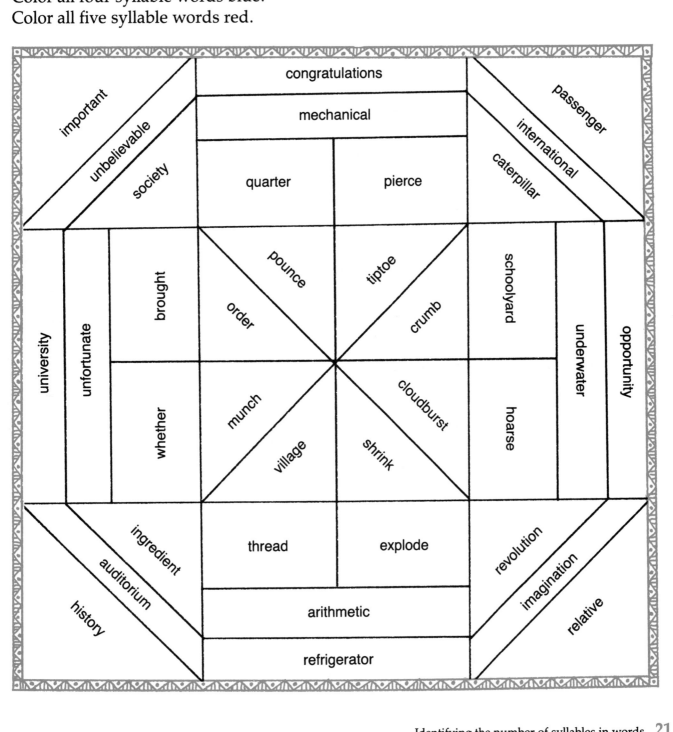

Syllable Sprint

Ask someone to play this game with you.
Make two small markers to use on the game board.
Write each player's name on a marker.
Take turns. Flip a coin on each turn.
Move your marker ahead two spaces for heads.
Move ahead one space for tails.
Read the word on which you land and count the number of syllables.
Move ahead one space for each syllable.
The first player to reach the finish line is the winner.

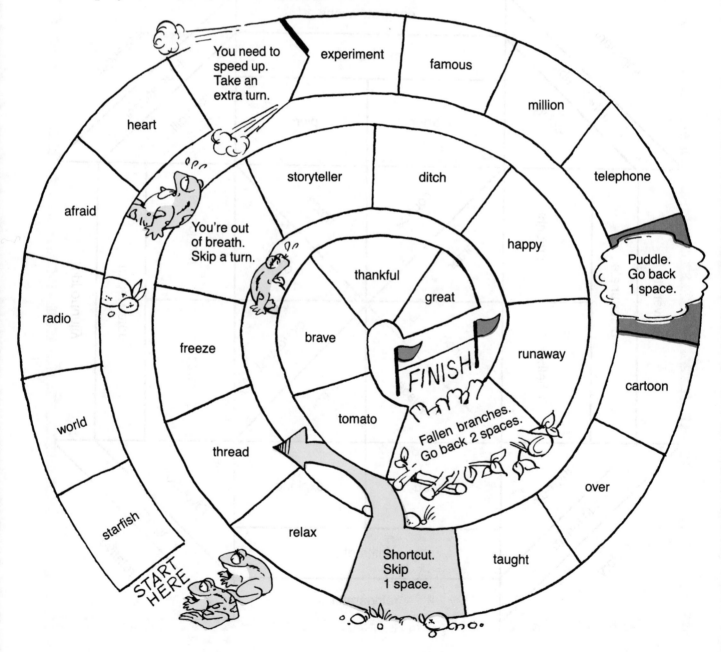

11 ▷ Sentence Scramble

Here are some scrambled sentences.
Unscramble each sentence by putting the words in alphabetical order.
Write the new sentence on the line.
Then suppose the words in each sentence are on a dictionary page.
Choose the correct guide words for each page from the words in the box.
Write the guide words at the beginning and end of each sentence.

Guide Word Box

time	wring	curb	and
prove	crew	wrap	two
away	took	part	would
price	am	cave	tear
when	car	pail	aunt

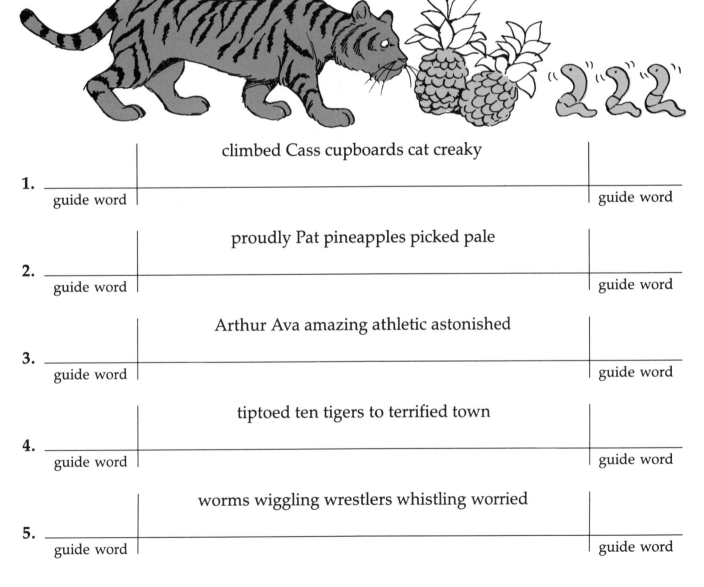

climbed Cass cupboards cat creaky

1. _____
   guide word | | guide word

proudly Pat pineapples picked pale

2. _____
   guide word | | guide word

Arthur Ava amazing athletic astonished

3. _____
   guide word | | guide word

tiptoed ten tigers to terrified town

4. _____
   guide word | | guide word

worms wiggling wrestlers whistling worried

5. _____
   guide word | | guide word

Look Around

Ask someone at home to do this activity with you.
Read the guide words on each dictionary page.
Work together.
Look around your home for objects whose names come
between the guide words on each page.
On each dictionary page, write the names of five objects you find.
Then number the words in alphabetical order.

bank / build

scale / swim

meal / my

fact / fuzz

Name _____

12 ▶ Entry Mix-Ups

Look at the dictionary pages below.
The parts of two dictionary entries are mixed up.
Sort out the entries.
Next to each picture, write the correct parts of the entry that
go with the picture.

The reindeer pulled the sleigh across the icy field.

noun

very pleasing to the senses of taste and smell

de·li·cious

(rān'dēr')

(di lish'əs)

The freshly baked bread smelled delicious.

rein·deer

adjective

a large deer with antlers that lives in cold, northern regions

entry word	pronunciation	part of speech

definition _____

_____

sample sentence _____

entry word	pronunciation	part of speech

definition _____

_____

sample sentence _____

Dictionary Disks

Play this game with a friend.

Make five playing cards like these.

Put the cards in a pile and turn the pile face down.

Take the top card.

Then toss a penny onto the game board.

Read what is written on the computer disk your penny lands on.

If what is written on the disk is an example of the part of a dictionary entry named on your card, score 5 points.

If you land on BUG or ERROR, lose 2 points.

Then return the card to the bottom of the pile.

Take turns and keep score on a piece of paper.

Play until one player scores more than 15 points.

entry word	pronunciation
part of speech	
definition	sample sentence

mem•o•ry	to feed information into a computer	(kəm pyōō'tər)	ERROR	We developed a program to help forecast the weather.
She put the floppy disk into the computer.	BUG	a gadget used to make choices on a computer screen	da•ta	adjective
a list showing what choices are available in a computer program	in•put	noun	He entered the names of all 50 states.	(kē'bôrd')
verb	(skrēn)	men•u	BUG	the part of a computer that stores information

Name _____

This is a map of a haunted house.

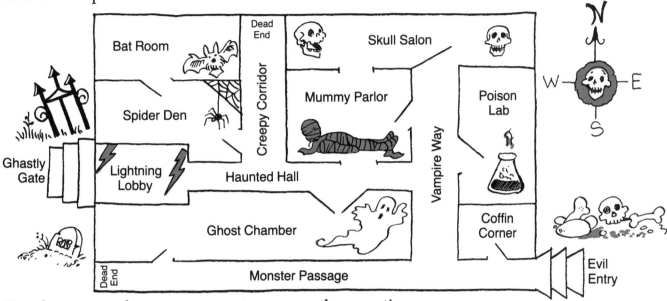

Use the map and map compass to answer the questions.

1. If you are brave enough to enter the house through the Ghastly Gate, what is the first room you come to? _____

2. You walk along the Haunted Hall and then along the Creepy Corridor. What is at the end of the Creepy Corridor? _____

3. You hear strange noises coming from the Bat Room. You want to investigate. Which room do you have to go through to get to the Bat Room? _____

4. You are chased into the Ghost Chamber through the double doors. You escape out the small door to the Monster Passage. If you want to hide in the Coffin Corner, in which direction should you run? _____

5. You have just left the Poison Lab after checking out the equipment. In which direction do you go on Vampire Way to get to the Skull Salon? _____

6. From the Skull Salon you can walk directly into which room? _____

7. After seeing all those mummies in the Mummy Parlor, you have had enough of this haunted house. You go out the door on Vampire Way and run south to the Monster Passage. Then you go east. Through what do you escape? _____

Word Count

Do this activity with an adult.

Choose one page in any book.

Look for these six words which are used most often in books.

    a   and   in   of   the   to

Count the number of times you find each word and tally the words below.

Stop when you get to the bottom of the page or when you have counted 20 of one of the words.

Then record your results on the bar graph.

Fill in the spaces above each word to show how many times the word was used.

a	and	in	of	the	to

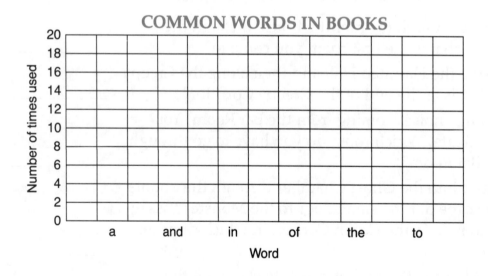

COMMON WORDS IN BOOKS

Which word was used most often? _____

Which word was used least often? _____

Do another word count and graph on a separate sheet of paper.
Use another book or a different page in the same book.

Was the same word used most often? _____

Was the same word used least often? _____

14 ▷ Cross Out

Read each paragraph.
All the sentences but one are about the same idea.
Find the sentence that does not belong and cross it out.

Stephanie Mills was singing almost before she could talk. She would sing with the radio, sing to her family, and sing with her friends. She liked to imagine she was a movie director or an orchestra conductor. Her parents sent her to acting school for professional training, and eventually she got a part in a Broadway show. Stephanie's older sister was also an actress. But Stephanie didn't become a Broadway star until she was 13 and she won the part of Dorothy in a show called *The Wiz*. She played the part for four years, and it was the beginning of her career as a famous singer.

One day in 1956, twelve-year-old Bobby Fischer visited the Manhattan Chess Club. He had never played there before, but he felt sure he could beat even the best players in the room. Once Bobby played on a park bench through a rainstorm. Bobby started to play, and a few people came over to watch. Then more people crowded around to watch Bobby make his moves. These men and women were experienced players, yet they were amazed at how brilliantly Bobby played. Little did they know that two years later Bobby would be the chess champion of the United States.

Reid Rondell trained for more than a year in order to be strong enough for the rough and tumble job of doing stunts. Then, when he was ten, Reid began his career as a stunt person. He does things in movies and TV shows that are too dangerous for the actors to do. Reid also likes to surf and water ski. He practices his stunts over and over so that everything is planned out before the stunt is performed. On screen, it looks like the actors are falling off horses, crashing cars, or jumping off mountains. But in reality, stunt people like Reid are doing these things.

Betty Bennett was just ten years old when she made her first solo airplane flight. Her father sold airplanes and there was an airfield behind her house. She sat in the plane by herself and waited for the engine to warm up. Then she gave the engine more gas, and the plane began to roll forward. It moved slowly at first. Then it raced faster down the runway. Finally the plane lifted into the air like a bird, gliding up into the sky. Betty swooped through the air over blue water. She circled over green fields and forests. When it was time to return, she drifted to the ground in a perfect landing.

What do all the paragraphs above tell about? _____

_____

What's It All About?

Here is an activity for three or more people.
Take turns reading a paragraph aloud.
As a group, discuss what the paragraph is about.
Then decide what the main idea is.
Write the main idea on the lines below the paragraph.

Unlike human workers, robots can work non-stop for long periods. They never get tired, and they always work with the same exactness. They can also work under conditions that humans could not bear, where it is very hot, very noisy, or where there are dangerous rays.

_____

_____

Franklin Pierce was President from 1853 to 1857. He wanted to take over Hawaii, which was still independent, but nothing came of it. He tried to buy Cuba from Spain, but that only made Spain angry. But he did manage to buy a narrow strip of land from Mexico. Today this forms part of New Mexico and Arizona.

_____

_____

Do you like fruits and vegetables? Well, how about digging into a watermelon that weighs 270 pounds? Or an orange the size of a human head? What about a peanut almost four inches long? Or an onion as big as a basketball? People have actually grown these large foods, and most of the foods have won prizes.

_____

_____

Some small insects live for only a few hours or days. At the other extreme, a tortoise may live for 150 years or more. Some plants, especially trees, live much longer. There are giant sequoia trees in California that began life almost 4000 years ago and some pine trees that are as old as the ancient pyramids.

_____

_____

A star lasts many millions of years, but eventually the gases inside it start to break down. This causes great heating, and the star swells up like a balloon, creating a red giant star. Much material is lost to space. Finally the red giant shrinks and becomes a cold, white dwarf star.

_____

_____

Your brain is in charge of everything. It makes sure your body is breathing, hearing, moving, feeling, and performing hundreds more tasks without you even noticing. Even while you are asleep, your brain is on duty, keeping you breathing and making sure all the parts of your body are working together.

_____

_____

Name _____

 Ghost Town

Some modern-day explorers discovered a western ghost town.
They made this chart to show what they discovered.

EXPLORATION OF WEST RANGE JUNCTION

Place Discovered	Dates Explored	Objects Found	Information About Citizens
General Store	September 10–12	herb jars flour sack	Owned by Mr. and Mrs. Bridges
Gold Mine	October 14–17	gold flakes panning equipment mining tools	Operated by G. Lawrence
Jail	October 11–13	sheriff's badge handcuffs	Outlaws killed Sheriff Marks in 1831
Schoolhouse	September 7–8	slate readers	Miss Hastings taught for 25 years

Use the chart to answer the following questions.

1. Which place was explored first? _____

2. Who owned the general store? _____

3. Which places were explored in October? _____

4. What objects were found in the general store? _____

5. Who killed Sheriff Marks? _____

6. In which place were the most objects found? _____

7. Which citizen helped children learn to read? _____

What do you think was the purpose of the exploration?

_____

_____

All About Me

Ask a family member to help you with these activities.

My Numbers

You can describe yourself with numbers.
Choose eight of the items listed below.
Fill in the circle in front of each item you choose.
Then have your family member help you find the numbers.
Write each number after the item.

○ length of nose _____   ○ number of T-shirts _____

○ length of thumb _____   ○ number of pairs of sneakers _____

○ length of little toe _____   ○ how long it takes to count to 100 _____

○ length of hair _____   ○ how long can hold breath _____

○ length of foot _____   ○ how long it takes to brush teeth _____

○ time born _____   ○ how long it takes to say alphabet _____

○ lucky number _____   ○ how far can jump _____

Rectangle or Square?

You can also describe yourself as a shape.
Get a ball of string and a pair of scissors.
Have your family member cut a piece of string equal
to your height.
Then cut a piece as long as your outstretched arms.
Compare the pieces of string.
If one is longer than the other, you are a rectangle.
If they are the same length, you are a square.
Write your name in the rectangle or square to show
which shape you are.

Consider the new things you learned about yourself.
Which three things were most surprising?

Rectangle

Square

_____   _____   _____

If your friends or other family members are interested, help
them find out their numbers and shapes.

16 Time Trip

A newspaper reporter living in the year 2100 took a trip back in time.
The reporter wrote an article about the trip.
Read the article.
Then complete the items at the end.

THE LOSHAR NEWS

On my last vacation, I decided to take a trip back in time. I went back more than a century and visited the United States in the year 1991.

Of course I saw many strange and unusual things. What surprised me most, though, was how the people entertain themselves. What seems to be their favorite entertainment involves the use of a large box-shaped container. The container either stands on legs or rests on a table or shelf. On one side of the container, the side people look at, is a piece of glass. Nearby, either on the container, a separate panel, or a hand-held pad, are the controls. When you operate the controls, the glass lights up in several colors. Images parade across the glass. Music and speech come forth. People spend hours watching and listening to their container. They laugh at the container, they talk about it, and generally seem to just adore it.

1. Write four important details from the article that describe the object or explain how it works.

   _____

   _____

   _____

   _____

2. What object or activity is the reporter writing about?

   _____

3. Write a headline for the article.

   _____

4. Draw a picture of the object in the space to the right of the article.

Missing Parts

Work together with a friend.
Complete each paragraph by filling in the blanks.
Use the part of speech written below the blank or write a
sentence if it says "sentence."
Be as silly as you like and have fun.
When you are finished, read the paragraphs aloud.

No one had ever seen a talking hamster before, but the _____
                                                                    adjective

_____ hamster just _____ and _____ all
        adjective   verb   verb

day long. Only its friend the _____ seemed to care, and it said so
                                        noun

quite _____. "_____
              adverb   sentence

_____," it complained.

Many years ago, a very timid dragon lost its way in a(n) _____. First
                                                                      noun

it _____, but that didn't help at all. So the dragon _____
            verb   verb

and _____ to try to scare away the huge _____ in the
              verb   noun

nearby _____. But when the people saw the _____
                noun   adjective

_____ dragon coming, all they could say was, "_____!"
        adjective   interjection

This is the tale of a(n) _____ who _____ whenever it
                                  noun   verb

_____ a(n) _____. Now most people had never seen
          verb   noun

a(n) _____ _____, so no one paid any attention when
          adjective   noun

a(n) _____ _____ _____ onto the road.
          noun   verb   adverb

Finally it _____ _____ and _____ the
                    verb   adverb   verb

_____ _____.
        adjective   noun

17 ▶ Story Match

Read the story on the left and find the sentence on the right that tells what happened next.
Use a ruler to connect the dots between the parts that go together.

Rosa put on her sweat suit and running shoes. She jumped and stretched to warm up. Rosa was in good shape today.

Oscar put a worm on a hook and dropped his fishing line into the water. The hook floated down. Soon Oscar felt a tug on the line.

Jill helped Leah get her kite in the air. For a while the kite moved with the wind. Then Leah tripped and let go of the kite.

Agnes strummed her guitar. She tightened a string and then plucked it. Finally Agnes broke into song.

Ray fixed up his old bicycle. He cleaned and polished the frame and filled the tires with air. Then he set off down the road.

It was the hottest day so far this year. Kenzo decided to make a pitcher of lemonade. Then he set up a table at the roadside and put up a big sign.

It sailed high into the sky.

He had caught a giant fish.

He was sold out in less than an hour.

She jogged more than two miles.

A large group gathered to listen.

He went racing toward the lake.

W N A R P L T L R M E B E W A S D L U I O B C N

Circle all the letters not covered by a line.
Write the circled letters in order from top to bottom.

They spell the name of a delicious treat. _____

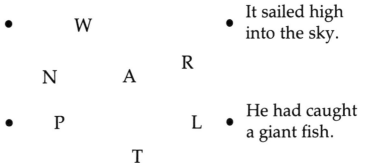
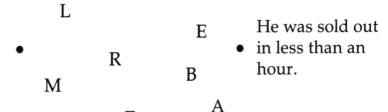
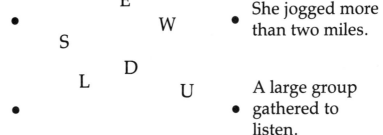
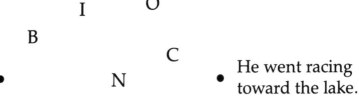

Round Robin

Do this activity with one or more friends.
Read the story beginnings below.
Choose the one you like best and circle it.
Read your choice aloud.
Then take turns adding a sentence to the story.
Keeping passing the story around until it is finished.
Each person may have several turns.
Continue on a separate sheet of paper if you need more room.
Read the story aloud when you are finished.

Princess Lella stood at the entrance to the cave. She gripped the magic sword more tightly. It seemed to grow hot in her hand.

"OK," José said as he pulled back the curtain. "This is it." Behind the curtain was the most wonderful contraption we had ever seen.

"Hey, cut that out," shouted a big, booming voice.
"What was that?" asked Murel.
"I'm the tree you just hit with your ax," came the reply.
"And I'm in no mood to be tickled."

We had heard about a giant creature that roamed the woods, but we didn't believe it really existed. Yet here we were, staring down at these *gigantic* footprints.

_____

_____

_____

_____

_____

_____

_____

Name _____

Read the title and author of each book.
Decide in which bookcase the book belongs.
Write the title of the book on a shelf in the bookcase.

A TRIP to the ZOO by Ann Immel

The Little People by To B. Tiny

Kids in the Kitchen by Watta Mess

SPORTS JOKES & RIDDLES by Make M. Laugh

HOW TO MAKE PIZZA by O. VEN

PLAY BALL! by Doug Out

What SWIMS in the OCEAN? by C. Greature

Cooking is Fun by U. Bakem

The LOST PRINCE by Ivan Togohome

BIRDWATCHER'S HANDBOOK by Burdon Thehand

Soccer for Everyone by Yul Kickim

Telephone Twins by Wee Callyou

Cooking	Animals	Sports	People

Which bookcase contains books most interesting to you? _____

Which book in that bookcase would you most like to read? _____

Story Sense

This is a game to play with an adult.
Copy the sentences below on a piece of paper.
Write each sentence on a separate line and leave space between the lines.
Cut between the sentences so that you have twelve sentence strips.
Mix up the strips.
Place them face up and end-to-end in two rows, one below the other.
Now take turns.
Change the position of any two sentence strips.
Read the story aloud from beginning to end.
If the story makes sense, you win.
If the story does not make sense, keep playing until it does.

I got up very early the next day.

I built a huge snowhouse.

It was very warm inside.

The ground was covered with snow.

I put on my warm winter clothes.

The weather report said it had also gotten warm outside.

All day long I played in my snowhouse.

I ran to look out the window.

My snowhouse had melted to the ground!

I got washed and took off my pajamas.

I ran out into the snow.

I woke up and looked out my window.

Name <u> </u>

 Consider the Facts

What can you figure out from each set of facts?
Circle the letter of the choice you think is most likely true.
When you are finished, compare your answers with your classmates.
Discuss why you chose each answer.

Fact Set 1

A girl lost her baseball.
She threw it so hard it went over the fence.

   a. The ball was actually a softball.
   b. The ball was caught on the other side of the fence.
   c. The ball could not be more than a mile away.

Fact Set 2

There was a sudden rainstorm.
There are footprints in the kitchen.

   a. Someone was wearing new shoes.
   b. Someone walked through the mud.
   c. Someone was caught without an umbrella.

Fact Set 3

It is twelve noon.
The front door of the building is locked.

   a. There is no one in the building.
   b. There is an open door in the back.
   c. There is no school on Saturday.

Fact Set 4

There is a clock on the wall.
Its hands are not moving.

   a. The clock will show the same time in five minutes.
   b. The clock is missing some parts.
   c. The clock fell off the wall the day before.

Fact Set 5

An animal escaped from the zoo.
It squeezed through bars that were two feet apart.

   a. The animal escaped at night.
   b. The animal was a black seal.
   c. The animal was not an elephant.

Fact Set 6

Two lamps were turned on.
The room was still quite dark.

   a. The lamps were very old.
   b. The light bulbs had burned out.
   c. The lamp shades were dark blue.

Guess Where

Ask a friend to help you take this challenge.
Do not read below the dotted line.
Have your friend read each list to you one sentence at a time.
After you hear each sentence, take one guess at where you are.
Have your friend tell you if you are right or wrong.
If you guessed wrong, go on to the next sentence.
If you guessed right, score 10 points minus 1 point for each sentence that was read to you.
Compute your score in the score box.
Try for a grand total of 15 points or more for all three places.

Place 1

1. People are cheering.
2. A horse is galloping around.
3. There are ropes above your head.
4. You can smell popcorn.
5. You are inside a tent.
6. You hear a lion roar.
7. You see acrobats and clowns.   ANSWER: CIRCUS

Score Box

10 − ☐ = ☐
            TOTAL

Place 2

1. Many people are wearing matching clothes.
2. Someone is throwing something.
3. People keep looking up in the air.
4. Some people are pushing each other.
5. Someone in a striped shirt is blowing a whistle.
6. There are tall metal posts nearby.
7. Someone is yelling, "Hike!"   ANSWER: FOOTBALL GAME

Score Box

10 − ☐ = ☐
            TOTAL

Place 3

1. A loud alarm is ringing.
2. People are rushing to get dressed.
3. The people are putting on coats, gloves, and boots.
4. Some people are putting on big helmets.
5. People are sliding down a pole.
6. Several large trucks are nearby.
7. The trucks are carrying ladders, hoses, and axes.

ANSWER: FIRE STATION

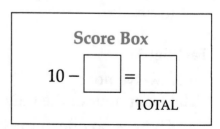

GRAND TOTAL _____

Name _____

20 ▶ Headlines

Read each newspaper headline.
Circle the statement that gives the probable reason for
the headline.

•The Record•
EXTRA

GIANT WAVES STRIKE COAST

earthquake in Colorado

tornado across Kansas

hurricane near Florida

• The NEWS •

Famous Actress Gone!

movie star changed name

new movie closed

movie star disappeared

THE GAZETTE

**TONS OF SNOW
ALL ROADS CLOSED**

snow shovelers strike

sudden winter storm

new highway construction

~ The Advance ~

New Crater Discovered on Moon

scientists using powerful new telescopes

astronauts training for space mission

pilots flying world's fastest airplane

Write a reason for this headline on
the newspaper.

The Sun

Dallas Knee-Deep in Sheep

explosion in sweater factory

escaped farm animals

people wearing shorts

Our Town News

"Noise Must Stop!" says Mayor

What Happened?

Play this game with someone in your family.
Cut out sixteen pieces of paper the size of the boxes below.
Place one piece of paper over each box.
Take turns.
Uncover one Cause box and one Effect box.
Read the cause and effect aloud.
If the cause and effect go together, leave the boxes uncovered and score 2 points.
If the cause and effect do not match, recover the boxes.
Keep score on a piece of paper.
The first player to score 10 points is the winner.

Cause

The waiter spilled tomato soup on me.	We mixed yellow and blue paint together.
Yoko pulled on the oars.	Stan blew into his trumpet.
Kerri plugged the cord into the wall.	Jake lost his eyeglasses.
The baby knocked over a glass of water.	A cold wind was blowing.

Effect

Colored lights lit up the room.	We heard a loud blast of sound.
There is a puddle on the floor.	He kept bumping into things.
We put on our warm coats.	There are red stains on my shirt.
We painted our doghouse green.	The boat glided through the water.

Name _____

Someone has robbed a bank.
Can you figure out who did it?
The signs the people are holding will give you clues.
After you read each clue, write the first letter of the clue on
the line at the bottom of the page.
Then do what the clue says.
Start by looking for the person who is not afraid of wild animals.

OUT OF LUCK. I DON'T HAVE TIME TO ROB BANKS. LOOK FOR THE PERSON WHO SAYS BALL GAMES ARE THE BEST SHOWS ON TV.

WHAT? I'M NOT THE PERSON YOU WANT. WHY DON'T YOU LOOK FOR THE PERSON WHO THINKS SUPERMARKETS ARE INTERESTING PLACES TO VISIT?

BANKS? I NEVER ROB THEM! TRY LOOKING FOR THE PERSON WHO SPENDS LOTS OF MONEY IN PAINT STORES.

WHY ASK ME? I'M NOT GUILTY. LOOK FOR THE PERSON WHO FEELS AT HOME ON THE RANGE.

YOU SOLVED THE CRIME! JUST READ THE SENTENCE AT THE BOTTOM OF THE PAGE TO FIND OUT WHO ROBBED THE BANK.

I DON'T WANT TO TALK ABOUT IT! LOOK FOR THE PERSON WHO IS ALWAYS TALKING ABOUT VEGETABLES.

OH, NO! I DIDN'T DO IT. YOU SHOULD LOOK FOR THE PERSON WHO IS REALLY GOOD AT SOLVING CRIMES.

COMPLETELY INNOCENT. MAYBE YOU SHOULD LOOK FOR THE PERSON WHO MOVES IN TIME WITH MUSIC.

The _____ did it.

What a Character!

Work with a friend or an adult.
Read each question.
Answer with the name of a person from books you have read.
You may both give the same answer or different answers.
Choose the left side or right side of the page.
Take turns writing your answers.

1. Who is the funniest person you have ever read about?

   _____   _____

2. Who is the meanest, most rotten person you have read about?

   _____   _____

3. If you had to spend a year on a deserted island with just
   one person, who would it be?

   _____   _____

4. Who is the biggest and strongest person you have read about?

   _____   _____

5. Who would you have a lot of trouble keeping quiet in a library?

   _____   _____

6. Which person reminds you a lot of yourself?

   _____   _____

7. If you could interview anyone on your list, who would it be?

   _____   _____

8. Write three questions you would ask that person.

   _____   _____

   _____   _____

   _____   _____

22 ▸ Picture This

Words can be used to create images, or pictures, in your mind.
Several items are named below.
Picture each item in your mind.
Then circle the letter of the choice that does *not* help you
create an image of the item.

1. an underground cave

   b. darkness
   c. mist
   d. cobwebs
   e. wrinkles

2. a crowded beach

   m. sand castles
   n. falling leaves
   o. colored towels
   p. plastic shovels

3. a car factory

   e. assembly lines
   f. glowing hot metal
   g. palm trees
   h. wheels and doors

4. a jungle

   i. long icicles
   j. warm rain
   k. hanging vines
   l. swarming bugs

5. a library

   l. quiet people
   m. shelves and tables
   n. tennis balls
   o. daily newspapers

6. a carnival

   d. funny performers
   e. frozen dinners
   f. flashing lights
   g. colorful balloons

7. a garbage dump

   b. old papers
   c. noisy trucks
   d. tin cans
   e. new shoes

8. an apple orchard

   q. crisp fruit
   r. clean windows
   s. rows of trees
   t. overloaded baskets

9. a rock band

   s. typewriters
   t. crazy dancing
   u. microphones
   v. loud singing

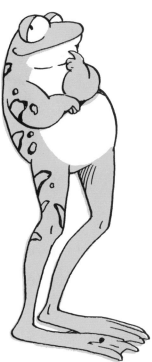

Can you picture a funny answer to this question?
Write the letters of your choices in order and
"see" what you get.

Q How do trains hear?

A They use their _____.

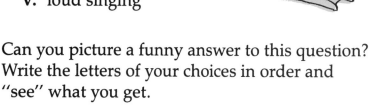

Mind Reader

Here is an activity for you and a friend.
Take turns.
Choose one item from the item box.
On separate paper, list ten words or phrases that would help
you create an image of the item.
Do not show your list to your friend.
Now tell your friend the name of the item.
Have your friend make his or her own list of ten words or phrases.
Compare your lists.
Score 1 point for each word or phrase that is on both lists.
Record your score below.
Do the activity for six different items.

Item Box

popcorn	ocean	garden
submarine	lamb	blizzard
old shoes	marching band	motorcycle
telephone	burning building	scarecrow

Item 1	
Item 2	
Item 3	
Item 4	
Item 5	
Item 6	
TOTAL SCORE	

Check How You Did

If your total score is

9 points or less, you could do better.

10–21 points, you are getting warmer.

22–35 points, you are tuned in.

36 points or more, you are mind readers!

Name _____

Read each question.
Write your answers on the lines.
When you are finished, compare your answers with
your classmates.

1. If you dug straight down from the ground, what four
   things would you probably find?

   _____   _____

   _____   _____

2. If you went to the doctor because you felt very hot, what
   four things would the doctor probably do?

   _____   _____

   _____   _____

3. If you were to spend a week on a deserted island, what
   four things would you need to bring along?

   _____   _____

   _____   _____

4. If you visited a museum, what four different things might
   be on display?

   _____   _____

   _____   _____

5. If you were to be a teacher for one day, what four things
   would you need in class?

   _____   _____

   _____   _____

Strange Situations

Ask a friend to do this activity with you.
Four strange situations are given below.
Read each question.
Work together to decide on your answers.
Write your answers on the lines.

1. If you could build a farm on the moon, what three things would it have that most other farms have?

   _____

   _____

   _____

   what three things would it have that *no* other farm has?

   _____

   _____

   _____

2. If you were only three inches tall, what three new things would you be able to do?

   _____

   _____

   _____

   what three things would you *not* be able to do?

   _____

   _____

   _____

3. If you could train an elephant to compete in the Olympics, which two events would it probably win?

   _____

   _____

   in which two events would it come in last?

   _____

   _____

4. If it snowed on the 4th of July, what two things would you be unable to do?

   _____

   _____

   what two things could you do for the first time ever?

   _____

   _____

Now work together to make a poster for one of the situations.
Include pictures showing your answers to the questions.
Take your poster to school tomorrow and show it to your classmates.

24 Follow the Plan

The plan below will help you write a story.
Choose one or more characters from the character box, or make up your own characters.
Name the characters and write their names on the line provided.
Next choose a place from the place box, or use a place you like better.
Write the name of the place on the first line of "Setting."
Now think about what will happen in your story.
Fill in the rest of the story plan with your ideas.

Character	
firefighter	ghost
robot	ballplayer
dragon	singer

Place	
volcano	fireworks show
Africa	movie studio
toy store	sunken ship

1. **Characters** _____

2. **Setting** Where the story takes place _____

   When the story takes place _____

3. **Problem** What needs to be worked out _____

   _____

4. **Goal** What the characters want to accomplish _____

   _____

5. **Action** Events in the story _____

   _____

   _____

   Reactions to the events _____

   _____

6. **Outcome** Results of the events and reactions _____

   _____

Now write a story based on your story plan.
Write your story on separate paper.
When you are finished, share your story with your classmates.

Story Map

Do this activity with an adult.
Get a copy of one of your favorite stories.
If the story is short, read the entire story for this activity.
If the story is long, use just one or two chapters.
Write the title and author on the line below.
Then take turns reading the story aloud page-by-page.
After a page is read, fill in whatever you can on the story map.
Use the completed map to retell the story in your own words.

Story map for _____ by _____.

Characters

Setting (time, place)

Problem (what needs to be worked out)

Goal (what characters want to accomplish)

Action (events, reactions)

Outcome (results of Action)

25 ▸ Know Your Planets

A fact is something that can be counted, checked, or tested.
An opinion is what someone thinks or feels about something.
Read each statement.
Circle **F** for *fact* or **O** for *opinion*.

1. Neptune rotates once every 18 to 20 hours.   **F   O**

2. Venus is named for the Roman goddess of love and beauty.   **F   O**

3. The planets are the most beautiful objects in the sky.   **F   O**

4. Mars is sometimes called the Red Planet.   **F   O**

5. A day on Mercury is equal to 59 days on Earth.   **F   O**

6. The planets do not produce their own heat and light.   **F   O**

7. Uranus is not a very interesting planet.   **F   O**

8. Visitors from Mars have probably landed on Earth.   **F   O**

9. Saturn is surrounded by thousands of rings formed of ice.   **F   O**

10. Pluto is the smallest of all the planets.   **F   O**

11. Looking at the planets through a telescope is fun.   **F   O**

12. One of Jupiter's moons has erupting volcanoes.   **F   O**

13. Everybody ought to know the names of the planets.   **F   O**

14. The atmosphere of Venus is filled with thick clouds.   **F   O**

What do you know about Earth?
Write three facts.

_____

_____

_____

Now write three opinions you have about Earth.

_____

_____

_____

Money, Money

Ask someone to play this game with you.
Take turns.
Choose one statement below and read it aloud.
Decide whether it is a fact or an opinion.
Then use a nickel to check if you are right.
Put the nickel on the shape in the box.
If it completely covers the shape, the statement is a fact.
If some part of the shape shows, the statement is an opinion.
Keep track of how many times you are right.
Do not reuse any boxes.
The first player to be right six times is the winner.

Abraham Lincoln is on the penny.	75¢ is a lot of money.	$1 bills wear out in about 18 months.	All coins contain some copper.
The $2 bill has a nice picture on the back.	A half dollar is worth more than a quarter.	Pennies are the best coins.	It is a good idea to save money.
A quarter has ridges around the edge.	Coin collecting is an interesting hobby.	Paper money is easier to use than coins.	A nickel is bigger than a dime.
A dollar is worth 100 cents.	Paper money is printed on special paper.	A coin is dated with the year it was made.	The United States should use only coins.

Name _____

People who write ads want you to buy or do something.
They use special ways of writing to convince you.
Look at the pictures below.
Each person works for a different company.
Read what each person is saying.

WE ALWAYS LIKE TO MENTION A FAMOUS PERSON IN OUR ADS.

THE ADS WE CREATE GIVE THE IMPRESSION THAT EVERYBODY HAS THE PRODUCT.

IN OUR ADS WE REPEAT THE NAME OF THE PRODUCT SEVERAL TIMES.

FOR OUR ADS, WE USE THE WORDS OF SOMEONE WHO HAS THE PRODUCT.

Creative Copy
Company

Sell Well
Productions

Ads
Unlimited

Words That
Work, Inc.

Now read each advertisement.
Find the person who describes the way the ad was written.
Write the name of the person's company on the line below the ad.

My soggy breakfast cereal was getting me down. Same old mush every morning. Then I tried new Crisp O's, and my mornings came alive. Each delicious little piece stays crispy and crunchy until I gobble it up. So if you're like me and tired of mush in the morning, try new Crisp O's. You'll be glad you did.

_____

What is everyone talking about these days? What is everyone buying? Our new Song Saver Super System! Best way to organize your records and cassettes. These systems are selling quickly. Don't *you* be left out. Get yours today!

_____

Need a new hair style? Want to look like a movie star? Come to Snip and Clip, the only choice for the best and latest in hair styles. Curly Locks, well-known movie and TV star, never looks better than after a trip to our shop. So visit Snip and Clip soon for hair like the stars.

_____

Hopping Hitops. The only sneakers you'll need. Hopping Hitops. You'll jump higher. You'll run faster. Hopping Hitops put bounce and spring in your step. Hopping Hitops. Get a pair soon and hop, hop, away.

_____

Advertise!

Do this activity with a friend.
The names of some products are given in the box.
Choose one for which you would like to write an
ad, or make up your own product.
Work together to make notes for your ad.
Fill in the note card below.

Invisible Ink	Spaghetti Hook
Music Computer	Shadow Saver
Auto Skates	Bubble Chamber
Truth Machine	Crayon Melter

NOTES FOR ADVERTISEMENT

Product Name

Ways to Write About Product

1. Suggest Everybody Has Product

2. Repeat Product Name

3. Name Famous Person

4. Use Words of Person Who Has Product

Now work together to write your advertisement.
Use one or more of the ideas you wrote on the note card.
Work on separate paper until you get your ad just right.
Then write the final ad here.
You may also draw a picture of the product and attach it to
the ad.
Take your ad to school tomorrow and read it to your classmates.

_____

_____

_____

_____

_____

Name _____

Read each sentence.
Search for the missing word in the puzzle.
Look across, down, and on a slant.
Circle the word and write it in the sentence.

1. Polar bears live on the floating ice of

   _____ regions.

2. When a _____ erupts,
   blazing lava pours down its slopes.

3. Your _____ is a frame of
   bones that gives your body its shape.

4. In 1969, the first astronauts walked

   on the _____.

5. A _____ is the stony
   remains of an ancient animal.

6. Scientists study the clouds to forecast

   the _____.

7. The _____ over the lake
   kept us from seeing the other shore.

8. _____ is a way of sending
   sounds through space.

9. The rocket shot a _____
   into orbit around the earth.

10. Light forms an image on the inner

    surface of your _____.

11. A grasshopper is an _____
    with strong legs for jumping.

s	a	t	e	l	l	i	t	e
k	v	o	l	c	a	n	o	f
e	a	r	l	b	r	s	e	o
l	m	r	a	t	c	e	f	s
e	e	o	i	d	t	c	o	s
t	y	n	o	s	i	t	g	i
o	t	e	e	n	c	o	i	l
n	n	w	e	a	t	h	e	r

Write the leftover letters from the puzzle.
Go in order across each row from top to bottom.
They spell the name of a famous scientist.

— — — — — — —   — — — — — — — —

Famous Leaders

This is a game for two players.

Take turns.

Close your eyes and put a finger on the game board.

Read what the person you are pointing to is saying.

Then try to discover where the person lived.

The name of the place is hidden in what the person is saying.

The person's home will be one of the places given below.

If you find the name of the place, circle it in the person's speech.

If you point to a person whose home has already been found, take another turn.

Play until all the people's homes have been found.

China	Germany	Greece	India	Rome	USA

I ruled all of Europe, from east to west.

Augustus Caesar

The great wall that surrounds my country has not changed much in a thousand years.

Confucius

I led my country in a revolution that made us an independent country.

George Washington

I did not worry if it would anger many people when I helped make my country rich and powerful.

William II

With peace in mind I aided my country's struggle for independence.

Mahatma Gandhi

I thought my form of government was best. Thomas Jefferson seemed to agree, centuries later. He made his country a democracy, also.

Pericles

Name _____

28 ▷ The Story of ?

A biography is the written story of a person's life.
Answer the questions below.
They will help you get started on a biography of an
imaginary person.

1. What is your imaginary person's name?

_____

2. When was the person born?

_____

3. Where does the person live?

_____

4. What does the person look like?

_____

5. What are the person's favorite foods?

_____

6. What are the names of the person's best friends?

_____

7. What does the person do during the day?

_____

8. What are the names of the people in the person's family?

_____

Now that you know some things about
your imaginary person, write a story
about a funny day in the person's life.
Write your story on separate paper.
Then draw a picture of your person in
the picture frame.
Share your story and picture with your
classmates.

My Time Line

Ask an adult in your home to help you with this activity.
Answer each question below about yourself.
Then draw an arrow to the time line to show your age when
you did each thing.

Time Line

1. When and where were you born?

   _____ ● ——————→ ▪ 0 years old

2. When did you get your first tooth?

   _____ ● ▪ 1 year old

3. When did you start to walk?

   _____ ● ▪ 2 years old

4. When did you say your first word? What was it?

   _____ ● ▪ 3 years old

5. When did you start school?

   _____ ● ▪ 4 years old

   ▪ 5 years old

6. When did you first read a book by yourself?
   What was it about?

   ▪ 6 years old

   _____ ●

7. When did you first make yourself a sandwich?
   What kind was it? ▪ 7 years old

   ▪ 8 years old

   _____ ●

8. When did you first go somewhere by yourself?
   Where did you go? ▪ 9 years old

   ▪ 10 years old

   _____ ●

9. What was the best thing that happened to you? ▪ 11 years old

   _____ ● ▪ 12 years old

Now use some of the information above to write a true story
about your life.
Write your story on separate paper.
Then read your story to your family.
Ask if they can add any details you did not remember.
Add these details to your story and make a final copy.

Name _____

Real or Make-Believe?

The paragraphs below are all from the same story.
Read each paragraph.
Then write your answer to the question at the end.

The next morning, Jane stayed in her room and Mark stayed in his room. In the room they shared, Katherine and Martha hardly talked at all. Each of the children was too busy making private plans.

Breakfast was eaten in silence, but not without the exchange of some excited looks. The children's mother was aware that something was in the air, and wondered what new trial lay in store for her.

Do you think this is a real-life
story or a make-believe story? _____

When their mother had gone to work and the dishes and other loathly tasks were done, the four children gathered in Katherine and Martha's room. Katherine had already checked to see that the charm still lay in its cubbyhole, unharmed by wish of mouse or termite.

Now, do you think this is a real-life
story or a make-believe story? _____

Jane had drawn up some rules.

"The wishes are to go by turns," she said. "Nobody's to make any main wish that doesn't include all the rest of us. If there have to be any smaller wishes later on in the same adventure, the person who wished the main wish gets to make them, except in case of emergency. Like if the person loses the charm and one of the other ones finds it."

What do you think now? Is this a
real-life story or a make-believe story? _____

Would you like to find out what happens to Jane, Mark, Katherine, and Martha?
You can find out in the book *Half Magic* by Edward Eager.
Look for it in your school or public library or a bookstore.

What's the Story?

Do this activity with a friend.
Some parts of a story are given below.
Read all the parts.
Then take turns adding sentences to fill in the missing parts.
Write your story so that the whole thing makes sense.
Use separate paper if you need more room to write.
Read the completed story aloud when you are finished.

One breezy summer day I was walking along the beach. Off in the distance I could just make out a dark spot on a sand dune. I walked closer to investigate. The dark spot turned out to be a wide, gaping hole. A light was shining far inside.

_____

_____

"Aha!" I heard echo off the walls. "You're looking for my treasure, aren't you?" I jumped in fright. By mistake, I ran further into the dune.

_____

_____

Luckily, I had a long rope in my backpack. I used it to climb out of the deep, sandy pit.

_____

_____

Everyone was gone, so I started to creep slowly and quietly back to the mouth of the dune. Then, suddenly, I heard a loud squawk.

_____

_____

I got out of there just in time. When I turned around, the hole in the sand dune had disappeared!

Name _____

Shape Poems

Here are some unusual poems to read.
The poems are shaped like what they tell about.

Hi, Ho! I'm headed over a high and mighty hilltop.

A fierce tornado is coming towards us. Run, run away!

Read the poems below.
Choose one and rewrite it in the shape of what it tells about.
Use the space to the right of the poems.

Rainbows
Red, green, blue, yellow, indigo.
Color explosion.

I wish I was a feather
Floating, floating in the wind.

A slimy snake
Slithering, sliding, slinking
Through the grass.

Now use your imagination to write your own shape poem.
Choose one of the shapes below, or use your own shape.
What does the shape make you think of?
On separate paper, write a shape poem about what you thought of.

Complete a Poem

Here is an activity for you and a friend.
Start by reading this poem aloud.
It will remind you of what you know about poetry.

> A poem is shorter than a story.
> It tells just one thought at a time.
> The words have a beat when you read them.
> And sometimes the words even rhyme.

Now work together to complete the poem below.
Work on two lines at a time.
The lines may rhyme or not, but try to use the same beat in both lines.
You can count the beats in each line by noticing which syllables are pronounced louder.
When the poem is finished, practice reading it aloud.
Take the poem to school tomorrow and read it to your classmates.

The clock _____

The time for _____

My friend _____

My friend and I _____

We thought we _____

We wished we _____

At last _____

But then _____

My friend and I _____

And now _____

Name _____

31 ▶ A Golden Tale

A myth is a made-up story about goddesses and gods.
The myth below is from ancient Greece.
Read the myth.
Then answer the questions at the end.

   In the land of Lydia there lived a king named Midas. Midas was not a
bad king, but he was rather greedy. He had a wife and a daughter who
loved him, and a lot of money, but he wanted to be even richer.
   One day King Midas did a favor for the god Dionysus. In return,
Dionysus told Midas he could make one great wish and it would come
true. So the king wished that everything he touched would turn to
gold. Dionysus granted the wish and King Midas was overjoyed.
   Everything was fine for a short while. The king touched some
flowers, and they turned into solid gold blossoms. He touched the
branch of a tree, and it turned into a precious golden object.
   Then the king had a terrible thought.
   "What will happen when I eat?" he wondered. Midas picked up an
apple. Before he could bite into it, it turned into gold. "I'll starve," the
king wailed. He knew then that he made an awful mistake. He started
to sob, and his daughter came to comfort him.
   "Stay away!" shouted Midas, but it was too late. When his daughter
gave him a hug she was turned into a shiny golden statue.
   The king was so full of grief that no one could console him. He
begged Dionysus to take away his power. Dionysus heard Midas and
granted his wish. Everything changed back to the way it was before,
but King Midas was no longer a greedy man. He had learned his lesson.

1. What lesson do you think King Midas learned from this experience?

_____

2. If someone says you "have the Midas touch," what do you
   think is meant?

_____

3. If you were King Midas, what would you have wished for?
   Why would you have made this wish?

_____

Chariot Race

Play this game with two friends or family members.
Make three small markers to use on the game board.
Then read about the Greek figures below.
Have each player choose a different one and write the name on a marker.
Take turns. Flip a coin on each turn.
If the coin comes up heads, move ahead one space.
If the coin comes up tails, move ahead two spaces.
The first player to land on FINISH is the winner.

ZEUS was king of all the gods. He lived high in the clouds and ruled the earth and sky. Sometimes he came down to the earth disguised as an animal.

- He commanded the rain and clouds.
- He could throw bolts of lightning.

ATHENA was the goddess of wisdom, bravery, and peace. She ruled over the useful and decorative arts of civilized life. The city of Athens is named for her.

- She wore a helmet, spear, and shield.
- She could tame wild horses.

POSEIDON was the ruler of the sea. He lived in a beautiful palace under the ocean. All the creatures that lived in the water were under his command.

- He controlled the oceans.
- He could cause violent earthquakes.

Enrichment
READING

Grade 4
Answer Key and Teaching Suggestions

AMERICAN EDUCATION PUBLISHING

OVERVIEW

ENRICHMENT READING is designed to provide children with practice in reading and to increase their reading abilities. The program consists of six editions, one each for grades 1 through 6. The major areas of reading instruction—word skills, vocabulary, study skills, comprehension, and literary forms—are covered as appropriate at each level.

ENRICHMENT READING provides a wide range of activities that target a variety of skills in each instructional area. The program is unique because it helps children expand their skills in playful ways with games, puzzles, riddles, contests, and stories. The high-interest activities are informative and fun to do.

Home involvement is important to any child's success in school. *ENRICHMENT READING* is the ideal vehicle for fostering home involvement. Every lesson provides specific opportunities for children to work with a parent, a family member, an adult, or a friend.

AUTHORS

Peggy Kaye, the author of *ENRICHMENT READING*, is also an author of *ENRICHMENT MATH* and the author of two parent/teacher resource books, *Games for Reading* and *Games for Math.* Currently, Ms. Kaye divides her time between writing books and tutoring students in reading and math. She has also taught for ten years in New York City public and private schools.

WRITERS

Timothy J. Baehr is a writer and editor of instructional materials on the elementary, secondary, and college levels. Mr. Baehr has also authored an award-winning column on bicycling and a resource book for writers of educational materials.

Cynthia Benjamin is a writer of reading instructional materials, television scripts, and original stories. Ms. Benjamin has also tutored students in reading at the New York University Reading Institute.

Russell Ginns is a writer and editor of materials for a children's science and nature magazine. Mr. Ginn's speciality is interactive materials, including games, puzzles, and quizzes.

WHY ENRICHMENT READING?

Enrichment and parental involvement are both crucial to children's success in school, and educators recognize the important role work done at home plays in the educational process. Enrichment activities give children opportunities to practice, apply, and expand their reading skills, while encouraging them to think while they read. *ENRICHMENT READING* offers exactly this kind of opportunity. Each lesson focuses on an important reading skill and involves children in active learning. Each lesson will entertain and delight children.

When childen enjoy their lessons and are involved in the activities, they are naturally alert and receptive to learning. They understand more. They remember more. All children enjoy playing games, having contests, and solving puzzles. They like reading interesting stories, amusing stories, jokes, and riddles. Activities such as these get children involved in reading. This is why these kinds of activities form the core of *ENRICHMENT READING*.

Each lesson consists of two parts. Children complete the first part by themselves. The second part is completed together with a family member, an adult, or a friend.

ENRICHMENT READING activities do not require people at home to teach reading. Instead, the activities involve everyone in enjoyable reading games and interesting language experiences.

Published in 1995 by AMERICAN EDUCATION PUBLISHING
© 1991 SRA/McGraw-Hill

HOW TO USE HOMEWORK READING

Each *ENRICHMENT READING* workbook consists of 31 two-page lessons. Each page of a lesson is one assignment. Children complete the first page independently. They complete the second page with a family member, an adult, or a friend. The two pages of a lesson focus on the same reading skill or related skills.

Each workbook is organized into four or five units emphasizing the major areas of reading instruction appropriate to the level of the book. This means you will always have the right lesson available for the curriculum requirements of your child.

The *ENRICHMENT READING* lessons may be completed in any order. They may be used to provide practice at the same time skills are introduced at school, or they may be used to review skills at a later date.

The games and activities in *ENRICHMENT READING* are useful additions to any classroom or home reading program. Beginning on page 68 you will find additional suggestions for classroom games and activities to follow up on the *ENRICHMENT READING* lessons.

Beginning on page 70 you will find the Answer Key for *ENRICHMENT READING*. In many cases, your child's answers will vary according to his or her own thoughts, perceptions, and experiences. Always accept any reasonable answers your child gives.

For exciting activities in mathematics, try . . .

ENRICHMENT MATH

By Peggy Kaye, Carole Greenes, and Linda Schulman

Grades 1 — 6

This delightful program uses a combination of games, puzzles, and activities to extend math skills acquired in the classroom to the real-life world of children and their families. Students using *Enrichment Math* will not be bored by the usual drill-and-practice exercises—they will actually *enjoy* doing their homework!

- Stimulating home activities reinforce classroom instruction in Number Meaning, Geometry, Measurement, and Problem Solving.
- Students become involved in active learning through practical applications of the math skills they learn in class.
- Pleasurable cooperative learning experiences foster positive student feelings about math and homework.
- Interaction among students and parents or other adults is encouraged throughout the program.
- *Enrichment Math* was written by three educators who know math and how children learn.

TEACHING SUGGESTIONS
Grade 4
Optional Activities

A TIP FOR SUCCESS

Children are sure to enjoy using Grade 4 of *ENRICHMENT READING* because it is filled with imaginative activities, games, and puzzles. Although the directions for each lesson are easy to read and understand, you may want to spend a few minutes reviewing them. Feel free to play the games and do the activities before assigning them. The games and activities will prepare children for success with their homework as well as provide them with reading experiences that appeal to their imaginations.

Vocabulary

The Vocabulary unit contains ten lessons designed to help children expand their vocabularies and build their general word knowledge. The first lesson focuses on synonyms and antonyms. After your child plays *Wonder Wheel* (page 4), you may wish to adapt the game for family use. Make a sturdy wheel out of cardboard, and have your child contribute words for the word cards. The number and selection of word cards can be varied each time the game is played.

Lessons 2 and 3 deal with prefixes and suffixes. To give children more practice using words with affixes, try this variation of a *Round Robin* story. Begin a story with a sentence that includes at least one word with a prefix and one word with a suffix. For example, "The submarine surfaced in the middle of an amusement park filled with extraterrestrial visitors." Have children take turns adding sentences to the story. Each sentence must include at least one word with a prefix and one word with a suffix. As an added challenge, ask children to include two or more prefixes and suffixes in each sentence.

People of all ages love riddles. After your child completes *Riddles* (page 11), you may want to start a home collection of riddles. Encourage children to contribute riddles in which the answers are dependent on the context of the questions. *Color Your Sentences* (page 13) also lends itself to some enjoyable family sharing. Have your child read his or her similes and metaphors aloud. Everyone will be surprised and delighted with the variety of answers. To encourage some imaginative artwork, have your child illustrate one or more of the comparisons on the page.

After children complete *Crosswords* (page 15) and *Ladder Climb* (page 16), they may want to try their hands at making up their own analogies. If your child need more practice in categorizing after completing *Wagon Wheels* (page 17), you may wish to have him or her complete additional category wheels. Some suggested categories for the wheel centers are weather, vehicles, book characters, writing instruments, fruits, and flowers.

Monster Poem (page 19) and *One Word Leads to Another* (page 20) give children opportunities to make simple semantic maps. After your child completes page 20, encourage him or her to share his or her answers with the family. You may all be surprised by how many different words the two pictures evoked.

Study Skills

The Study Skills unit contains three lessons covering dictionary skills, maps, and graphs. A thorough understanding of alphabetical order is crucial to developing good dictionary skills, but many children are bored by exercises that merely ask them to alphabetize words. *Sentence Scramble* (page 23) takes the boredom away. Children will have fun figuring out the scrambled sentences, and since the sentences turn out to be tongue twisters, they will delight in reading the sentences aloud. Children may also wish to make up their own alphabetic scrambled sentences for family members to figure out.

Another important dictionary skill involves becoming familiar with dictionary entries. *Entry Mix-Ups* (page 25) and *Dictionary Disks* (page 26) provide practice with this skill. After children play *Dictionary Disks*, they can make their own game boards for different topics. Have children make lists of words relating to their topics, look up the words in a dictionary, and then fill the boxes of their game boards with parts of the entries. When they play their games, children will be increasing their vocabularies as well as practicing their dictionary skills.

In *Haunted House* (page 27), children are required to use a map. To prepare for this activity, make sure your child is familiar with locating objects and places on a simple map. Also make sure your child is familiar with a map compass and where north, south, east, and west are located on a map. After your child completes page 27, he or she may enjoy making his or her own maps of real or imaginary places.

Before you assign *Word Count* (page 28), you may want to review with your child how to count items using tally marks and how to complete a simple bar graph. If your child finds this activity interesting, he or she may want to repeat it for the words *as, for, I, is, it, that* and/or for the individual letters of the alphabet.

Comprehension

The Comprehension unit contains twelve lessons covering the major aspects of comprehension appropriate to Grade 4. The first three lessons focus on finding main ideas and details. *Cross Out* (page 29) presents biographical paragraphs about four interesting youngsters. Children who express a particular interest in one or more of these youngsters might be encouraged to find out about their lives as adults. After children complete *All About Me* (page 32), they may enjoy comparing their results. Charts or graphs could also be made to record children's numbers and shapes. To extend *Time Trip* (page 33), challenge your child to describe other familiar objects in passages similar to that on page 33.

Children who recognize the play on words in the authors' names in *Where Does It Go?* (page 37) may enjoy making up additional book titles and authors to add to each bookcase. When your child works on *Consider the Facts* (page 39), encourage him to consider all the answer choices as he searches for reasons to disqualify them. *Guess Where* (page 40) and *What Happened?* (page 42) can easily be extended for home use by creating additional place descriptions and cause-and-effect sentences.

Several lessons require children to use their imaginations, rely on their own experiences and knowledge, and draw upon their previous reading experiences. Children are also asked to come up with original responses to open-ended questions. If children particularly enjoy *Mind Reader* (page 46), additional items may be added to the Item Box and a tournament or exhibition held at home.

In *Follow the Plan* (page 49), children are asked to complete a story plan and then write a story based on it. Be sure your child understands what kind of information should be included in each part of the plan, and provide help as needed if your child has difficulty organizing his or her ideas. Before *Story Map* (page 50), is assigned, you may want to introduce the activity at home and make sure children are familiar with how to complete the story map. The basic story map on page 50 may also be used whenever children read and analyze stories.

Forms of Writing

The Forms of Writing unit contains six lessons that help children develop appreciation for several different forms of written material including science, history, biography, fiction, and poetry.

Most children probably are not aware of persuasive writing techniques. To introduce Lesson 26, you may want to use some newspaper and magazine ads to help your child identify some of the persuasive techniques used. Once children become aware of this kind of writing, they will most likely find it everywhere.

After children complete *My Time Line* (page 58), they may find it interesting to compare their time lines and share their autobiographies. The activity may also spark an interest in time lines as a way of recording information. If children are interested, encourage them to make a variety of time lines, such as for their daily activities, school events, sports events, historical events, scientific events, and so on.

Shape Poems (page 61) encourages children to explore visual invention through the creation of poems shaped like what the poem tells about. In Lesson 31, children are introduced to some well-known Greek mythological figures. After children complete the lesson, you may wish to introduce them to some other myths. Children may also enjoy acting out a myth or reciting a myth in choral reading fashion.

Answer Key
Grade 4–Enrichment Reading

Page 3 Answers will vary.

Page 4 Words and results will vary.

Page 5

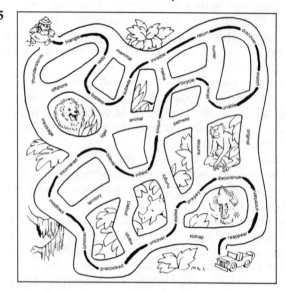

Page 6 Results will vary.

Page 7 beautify, painter, magician, workable, neighborhood, messy; answers will vary

Page 8 *Player 1:* discovery, fearless, generally, disappearance *Player 2:* disagreement, longest, studying, created

Page 9 1. bare 2. would 3. pane 4. weighs 5. write 6. one 7. for 8. find; blastoff

Page 10 *Top row:* pale, brakes, cent *Second row:* reign, steal, main *Third row:* scent, pail, breaks *Bottom row:* mane, rain, steel

Page 11 1. quackers 2. fired 3. barking 4. lions 5. syllable 6. diving 7. racket 8. squeak 9. Launch

Page 12 Meanings will vary.

Page 13 *Lines between:* Her eyes were–as big as pizzas. The kangaroo jumped–as high as the stars. The boxes were–as heavy as rocks. The thirsty boy–drank like a fish. The motor–sounds like a hive of bees. The light on the water–looks like diamonds. The ticking clock is–a time bomb. The little puppy is–a real clown. This room is–an oven.; answers will vary

Page 14 Descriptions will vary.

Page 15

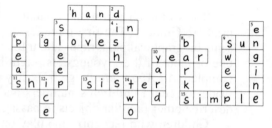

Page 16 *Player 1:* hear, insect, sing, brush, king, clean *Player 2:* fins, time, write, shape, breakfast, country

Page 17 *Top–possible answers:* animals or farm animals, tools *Bottom:* answers will vary

Page 18 Lists will vary.

Page 19 Poems will vary.

Page 20 Words will vary.

Page 21 *Orange:* pierce, brought, pounce, crumb, munch, shrink, hoarse, thread *Yellow:* quarter, order, tiptoe, schoolyard, whether, village, cloudburst, explode *Green:* important, passenger, history, relative *Blue:* society, mechanical, caterpillar, unfortunate, underwater, ingredient, arithmetic, revolution *Red:* unbelievable, congratulations, international, university, opportunity, auditorium, refrigerator, imagination

Page 22 Results will vary.

Page 23 1. car–Cass cat climbed creaky cupboards.–curb 2. pail–Pale Pat picked pineapples proudly.–prove 3. am–Amazing Arthur astonished athletic Ava.–away 4. tear–Ten terrified tigers tiptoed to town.–two 5. when–Whistling wiggling worms worried wrestlers.–wring

Page 24 Answers will vary.

Page 25 *Entry word:* de•li•cious *Pronunciation:* (di lish'əs) *Part of speech:* adjective *Definition:* very pleasing to the senses of taste and smell *Sentence:* The freshly baked bread smelled delicious.
Entry word: rein•deer *Pronunciation:* (rān'dēr') *Part of speech:* noun *Definition:* a large deer with antlers that lives in cold, northern regions *Sentence:* The reindeer pulled the sleigh across the icy field.

Page 26 Results will vary.

Page 27 1. Lightning Lobby 2. Dead End 3. Spider Den 4. east 5. north 6. Mummy Parlor 7. Evil Entry

Page 28 Results will vary, but most students should find the words are used most often in this order: *the, of, and, to, a, in.*

Page 29 *Crossed-out sentences:* Stephanie's older sister was also an actress. Once Bobby played on a park bench through a rainstorm. Reid also likes to surf and water ski. Her father sold airplanes and there was an airfield behind her house.; young people who have done unusual or interesting things

Page 30 *Robots:* Under some conditions, robot workers are better workers than humans. *Franklin Pierce:* President Pierce wanted to get more land for the United States. *Fruits and Vegetables:* Some people grow giant fruits and vegetables. *Insects:* The life-span of living things varies greatly. *Star:* A star does not last forever. *Brain:* Without your brain, you could not do anything.

Page 31 1. Schoolhouse 2. Mr. and Mrs. Bridges 3. Gold Mine, Jail 4. herb jars, flour sack 5. outlaws 6. Gold Mine 7. Miss Hastings; answers will vary

Page 32 Results and answers will vary.

Page 33 1. *Possible answers:* The object is a large box-shaped container. It stands on legs or rests on a table or shelf. One side of the container has a piece of glass that people look at. The container has controls. The controls make the glass light up in several colors. People watch images parade across the glass. Music and speech come from the container. 2. a television set or watching television 3. Headlines will vary, but should indicate the main idea of the article. 4. Pictures will vary, but should show a modern-day television set.

Page 34 Paragraphs will vary.

Page 35 *Lines between:* Rosa–She jogged more than two miles. Oscar–He had caught a giant fish. Jill–It sailed high into the sky. Agnes–A large group gathered to listen. Ray–He went racing toward the lake. Kenzo–He was sold out in less than an hour.; watermelon

Page 36 Stories will vary.

Page 37 Cooking: *Kids in the Kitchen, How to Make Pizza, Cooking is Fun* Animals: *A Trip to the Zoo, What Swims in the Ocean?, Birdwatcher's Handbook* Sports: *Sports Jokes & Riddles, Play Ball!, Soccer for Everyone* People: *The Little People, The Lost Prince, Telephone Twins*; answers will vary

Page 38 I woke up and looked out my window. The ground was covered with snow. I got washed and took off my pajamas. I put on my warm winter clothes. I ran out into the snow. I built a huge snowhouse. All day long I played in my snowhouse. I got up very early the next day. It was very warm inside. The weather report said it had also gotten warm outside. I ran to look out the window. My snowhouse had melted to the ground!

Page 39 *Fact Set 1:* c *Fact Set 2:* b *Fact Set 3:* c *Fact Set 4:* a *Fact Set 5:* c *Fact Set 6:* b

Page 40 *Place 1:* circus *Place 2:* football game *Place 3:* fire station; results will vary

Page 41 *The Record:* hurricane near Florida *The Gazette:* sudden winter storm *The Sun:* escaped farm animals *The News:* movie star disappeared *The Advance:* scientists using powerful new telescopes; reasons will vary

Page 42 Results will vary.

Page 43 cowboy

Page 44 Names and questions will vary.

Page 45 1. e 2. n. 3. g 4. i 5. n 6. e 7. e 8. r 9. s; engineers

Page 46 Answers and results will vary.

Page 47 Answers will vary.

Page 48 Answers and posters will vary.

Page 49 Ideas and stories will vary.

Page 50 Story maps will vary.

Page 51 1. F 2. F 3. O 4. F 5. F 6. F 7. O 8. O 9. F 10. F 11. O 12. F 13. O 14. F; facts and opinions will vary

Page 52 *Top row:* fact, opinion, fact, fact *Second row:* opinion, fact, opinion, opinion *Third row:* fact, opinion, opinion, fact *Bottom row:* fact, fact, fact, opinion

Page 53 *Crisp O's:* Words That Work, Inc. *Song Saver Super System:* Sell Well Productions, *Snip and Clip:* Creative Copy Company *Hopping Hitops:* Ads Unlimited

Page 54 Notes, ads, and pictures will vary.

Page 55 1. arctic 2. volcano 3. skeleton 4. moon 5. fossil 6. weather 7. fog 8. radio 9. satellite 10. eye 11. insect; Albert Einstein

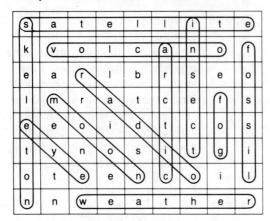

Page 56 *Augustus Caesar:* Rome *George Washington:* USA *Mahatma Gandhi:* India *Confucius:* China *William II:* Germany *Pericles:* Greece

Page 57 Answers, stories, and drawings will vary.

Page 58 Time lines and stories will vary.

Page 59 Answers may vary.

Page 60 Stories will vary.

Page 61 Shape poems will vary.

Page 62 Poems will vary.

Page 63 *Possible answers:* 1. He learned not to be greedy. 2. You probably are successful in all you do and make a lot of money from your activities. 3. answers will vary

Page 64 Results will vary.